Meatless

Publications International, Ltd.

Photograph on front cover (bottom) and page 61 copyright © Shutterstock.com.

Pictured on the front cover (top to bottom): Sweet Potato Maki Bowl (page 72) and Tofu and Sweet Potato Bowl (page 60).

Pictured on the back cover (clockwise from top left): Avocado Egg Rolls (page 122), Barbecue Cauliflower Calzones (page 42), Peanut Butter Tofu Bowl (page 68) and Creamy Tomato Soup (page 96).

ISBN: 978-1-64558-725-5

Manufactured in China.

8 7 6 5 4 3 2 1

Let's get social!
@Publications_International
@PublicationsInternational
www.pilbooks.com

TABLE
of
CONTENTS

Breakfast

CHEDDAR JALAPEÑO CORNMEAL WAFFLES

1¼ cups yellow cornmeal

¾ cup all-purpose flour

2 tablespoons sugar

2 teaspoons baking powder

1 teaspoon salt

½ teaspoon baking soda

¾ cup (3 ounces) shredded sharp Cheddar cheese

1 jalapeño pepper, sliced into thin rings

2 eggs

2 cups buttermilk

6 tablespoons butter, melted and slightly cooled

1. Preheat oven to 200°F. Preheat classic round waffle iron; grease lightly. Set wire rack on large baking sheet.

2. Whisk cornmeal, flour, sugar, baking powder, salt and baking soda in large bowl until combined. Fold in cheese and jalapeño pepper.

3. Whisk eggs in medium bowl. Add buttermilk and butter; whisk until well blended. Add to flour mixture; stir just until blended.

4. For each waffle, pour ½ cup batter into waffle iron. Close lid and bake 3 to 5 minutes or until steaming stops and waffle is golden brown and crisp. Remove to wire rack; keep warm in oven. Repeat with remaining batter.

Makes 8 servings

TIP

This is a great breakfast to make when you have leftover chili (like Quinoa Chili on page 100 or Sweet Potato and Black Bean Chipotle Chili on page 106). Reheat a little bit of chili and serve it with the waffles, some diced tomato and a dollop of sour cream or plain yogurt.

SWEET POTATO PANCAKES

2 medium sweet potatoes

2½ cups all-purpose flour

1 teaspoon baking powder

1 teaspoon baking soda

½ teaspoon salt

½ teaspoon ground cinnamon

¼ teaspoon ground ginger

2¾ cups buttermilk

2 eggs

2 tablespoons packed brown sugar

2 tablespoons butter, melted, plus additional for pan

Softened butter, maple syrup and/or chopped glazed pecans*

Glazed or candied pecans can be found in the produce section of the supermarket with other salad toppings, or they may be in the snack aisle.

1. Preheat oven to 375°F. Scrub sweet potatoes; bake 50 to 60 minutes or until soft. Cool slightly; peel and mash. Measure 1⅓ cups for pancake batter.

2. Combine flour, baking powder, baking soda, salt, cinnamon and ginger in medium bowl; mix well. Whisk buttermilk, eggs and brown sugar in large bowl until well blended. Stir in 2 tablespoons melted butter. Add sweet potato; whisk until well blended. Add flour mixture; stir just until dry ingredients are moistened and no streaks of flour remain. Do not overmix; batter will be lumpy. Let stand 10 minutes.

3. Heat griddle or large skillet* over medium heat; brush with additional melted butter to coat. For each pancake, pour ½ cup batter onto griddle, spreading into 5- to 6-inch circle. Cook about 4 minutes or until bottom is golden brown and small bubbles appear on surface. Turn pancake; cook about 3 minutes or until golden brown. Add additional butter to griddle as needed.

4. Serve pancakes topped with softened butter, maple syrup and/or pecans.

Makes 5 servings (10 large pancakes)

*Since pancakes are large, a skillet may not be able to cook more than one at a time. Keep cooked pancakes warm in 250°F oven on wire rack set over baking sheet.

CHEESY QUICHETTES

6 eggs

¼ cup whole milk

1½ cups thawed frozen shredded hash brown potatoes, squeezed dry

¼ cup chopped fresh parsley

½ teaspoon salt

1½ cups (6 ounces) shredded Mexican cheese blend or pepper-jack cheese

1. Preheat oven to 400°F. Spray 12 standard (2½-inch) muffin cups with nonstick cooking spray.

2. Whisk eggs in medium bowl until well blended. Whisk in milk. Add potatoes, parsley and salt; mix well. Spoon mixture evenly into prepared muffin cups.

3. Bake 15 minutes or until knife inserted into centers comes out almost clean. Sprinkle evenly with cheese; let stand 3 minutes or until cheese is melted. (Egg mixture will continue to cook while standing.) Gently run knife around edges and lift out with fork.

Makes 12 quichettes

BAKED APPLE PANCAKE

3 tablespoons butter

3 medium Granny Smith apples (about 1¼ pounds), peeled and cut into ¼-inch slices

½ cup packed dark brown sugar

1½ teaspoons ground cinnamon

½ teaspoon plus pinch of salt, divided

4 eggs

⅓ cup whipping cream

⅓ cup milk

2 tablespoons granulated sugar

½ teaspoon vanilla

⅔ cup all-purpose flour

1. Melt butter in 8-inch ovenproof nonstick or cast iron skillet over medium heat. Add apples, brown sugar, cinnamon and pinch of salt; cook about 8 minutes or until apples begin to soften, stirring occasionally. Spread apples in even layer in skillet; set aside to cool 30 minutes.

2. After apples have cooled 30 minutes, preheat oven to 425°F. Whisk eggs in large bowl until foamy. Add cream, milk, granulated sugar, vanilla and remaining ½ teaspoon salt; whisk until blended. Sift flour into egg mixture; whisk until batter is well blended and smooth. Set aside 15 minutes.

3. Stir batter; pour evenly over apple mixture. Place skillet on rimmed baking sheet in case of drips (or place baking sheet or piece of foil in oven beneath skillet).

4. Bake about 15 minutes or until top is golden brown and pancake is loose around edge. Cool 1 minute; loosen edge of pancake with spatula, if necessary. Place large serving plate or cutting board on top of skillet and invert pancake onto plate. Serve warm.

Makes 2 to 4 servings

FRITTATA RUSTICA

4 ounces cremini mushrooms, stems trimmed, cut into thirds

1 tablespoon olive oil, divided

½ teaspoon plus ⅛ teaspoon salt, divided

½ cup chopped onion

1 cup packed chopped stemmed lacinato kale

½ cup halved grape tomatoes

4 eggs

½ teaspoon Italian seasoning

Black pepper

⅓ cup shredded mozzarella cheese

1 tablespoon shredded Parmesan cheese

Chopped fresh parsley

1. Preheat oven to 400°F. Spread mushrooms on small baking sheet; drizzle with 1 teaspoon oil and sprinkle with ⅛ teaspoon salt. Roast 15 to 20 minutes or until well browned and tender.

2. Heat remaining 2 teaspoons oil in small (6- to 8-inch) nonstick skillet over medium heat. Add onion; cook and stir 5 minutes or until soft. Add kale and ¼ teaspoon salt; cook and stir 10 minutes or until kale is tender. Add tomatoes; cook and stir 3 minutes or until tomatoes are soft. Stir in mushrooms.

3. Preheat broiler. Whisk eggs, Italian seasoning, remaining ¼ teaspoon salt and pepper in medium bowl until well blended.

4. Pour egg mixture over vegetables in skillet; stir gently to mix. Cook about 3 minutes or until eggs are set around edge, lifting edge to allow uncooked portion to flow underneath. Sprinkle with mozzarella and Parmesan. Broil 3 minutes or until eggs are set and cheese is browned. Sprinkle with parsley.

Makes 2 servings

PECAN WAFFLES

2¼ cups all-purpose flour

3 tablespoons sugar

1 tablespoon baking powder

½ teaspoon salt

2 eggs

2 cups milk

¼ cup vegetable oil

¾ cup chopped pecans, toasted*

Butter and maple syrup for serving

To toast pecans, cook in medium skillet over medium heat 3 to 4 minutes or until lightly browned, stirring frequently.

1. Preheat classic round waffle iron; grease lightly.

2. Combine flour, sugar, baking powder and salt in large bowl. Whisk eggs in medium bowl until well blended. Whisk in milk and oil. Add to flour mixture; stir just until blended. Stir in pecans.

3. For each waffle, pour about ½ cup batter into waffle iron. Close lid and bake until steaming stops. Serve with butter and maple syrup.

Makes 8 waffles

FRENCH CARROT QUICHE

1 tablespoon butter

1 pound carrots, peeled and sliced into rounds

¼ cup chopped green onions

½ teaspoon herbes de Provence

1 cup milk

¼ cup whipping cream

½ cup all-purpose flour

2 eggs, beaten

½ teaspoon minced fresh thyme

¼ teaspoon salt

¼ teaspoon ground nutmeg

½ cup (2 ounces) shredded Gruyère or Swiss cheese

1. Preheat oven to 350°F. Grease four shallow 1-cup baking dishes or one 9-inch quiche dish or pie plate.

2. Melt butter in large skillet over medium heat. Add carrots, green onions and herbes de Provence; cook and stir 5 to 7 minutes or until carrots are tender.

3. Meanwhile, combine milk and cream in medium bowl; gradually whisk in flour. Stir in eggs, thyme, salt and nutmeg.

4. Spread carrot mixture in prepared dishes; top evenly with milk mixture. Sprinkle with cheese.

5. Bake 20 to 25 minutes for individual quiches (or 30 to 40 minutes for 9-inch quiche) or until firm. Serve warm or at room temperature.

Makes 4 servings

CRANBERRY WALNUT GRANOLA BARS

2 cups old-fashioned oats

¾ cup all-purpose flour

1 teaspoon pumpkin pie spice

½ teaspoon baking soda

½ teaspoon salt

1 cup packed brown sugar

¼ cup (½ stick) butter, softened

2 eggs

¼ cup orange juice

1 cup chopped walnuts

½ cup dried cranberries

1. Preheat oven to 350°F. Grease 9-inch square baking pan.

2. Combine oats, flour, pumpkin pie spice, baking soda and salt in medium bowl.

3. Beat brown sugar and butter in large bowl with electric mixer on medium-high speed until light and fluffy. Add eggs and orange juice; beat until blended. Gradually add oat mixture, beating on low speed just until mixed. Stir in walnuts and cranberries. Spread mixture in prepared pan.

4. Bake 20 to 25 minutes or until toothpick inserted into center comes out clean. Cool completely in pan. Cut into bars.

Makes 12 bars

TIP

To make this recipe vegan, substitute vegan plant butter for regular butter and flax for eggs (combine 2 tablespoons ground flaxseed and 6 tablespoons boiling water in small bowl; cool completely before using).

Salads

GREEK SALAD

SALAD

3 **medium tomatoes, cut into 8 wedges each and seeds removed**

1 **green bell pepper, cut into 1-inch pieces**

½ **cucumber (8 to 10 inches), quartered lengthwise and sliced crosswise**

½ **red onion, thinly sliced**

½ **cup pitted kalamata olives**

1 **block (8 ounces) feta cheese, cut into ½-inch cubes**

DRESSING

6 **tablespoons extra virgin olive oil**

3 **tablespoons red wine vinegar**

1 **to 2 cloves garlic, minced**

¾ **teaspoon dried oregano**

¾ **teaspoon salt**

¼ **teaspoon black pepper**

1. Combine tomatoes, bell pepper, cucumber, onion and olives in large bowl. Top with feta.

2. For dressing, whisk oil, vinegar, garlic, oregano, salt and black pepper in medium bowl until well blended. Pour over salad; stir gently to coat.

Makes 6 servings

BROCCOLI-RAISIN SALAD

SALAD

- **4 cups small fresh broccoli florets**
- **½ cup golden raisins or dried cranberries**
- **½ medium red onion, finely chopped**
- **¼ cup dry-roasted sunflower seeds**

DRESSING

- **¼ cup mayonnaise**
- **2 tablespoons milk**
- **1 tablespoon sugar**
- **2 teaspoons cider vinegar**
- **½ teaspoon salt**
- **Black pepper**

1. Combine broccoli, raisins, onion and sunflower seeds in large bowl.

2. For dressing, whisk mayonnaise, milk, sugar, vinegar and salt in medium bowl; season with pepper. Pour over broccoli mixture; mix well. Serve immediately or cover and refrigerate until ready to serve.

Makes 4 to 6 servings

TIP

To make this recipe vegan, use vegan mayonnaise instead of regular and substitute any unsweetened nondairy milk or water for the regular milk.

ZESTY ZUCCHINI CHICKPEA SALAD

3 medium zucchini (about 6 ounces each)

½ teaspoon salt

5 tablespoons white vinegar

1 clove garlic, minced

¼ teaspoon dried thyme

½ cup extra virgin olive oil

1 cup drained canned chickpeas

½ cup sliced pitted black olives

3 green onions, minced

1 canned chipotle pepper in adobo sauce, seeded and minced

1 ripe avocado, cut into ½-inch cubes

⅓ cup crumbled feta cheese

Lettuce leaves and sliced fresh tomatoes (optional)

1. Cut zucchini lengthwise into halves; cut halves crosswise into ¼-inch-thick slices. Place slices in medium bowl; sprinkle with salt. Toss to mix. Spread zucchini on several layers of paper towels. Let stand at room temperature 30 minutes to drain.

2. Combine vinegar, garlic and thyme in large bowl. Gradually whisk in oil until well blended. Pat zucchini dry; add to dressing. Add chickpeas, olives and green onions; toss lightly to coat. Cover and refrigerate at least 30 minutes or up to 4 hours, stirring occasionally.

3. Stir chipotle pepper into salad just before serving. Add avocado and cheese; toss lightly to mix. If desired, line shallow bowls or small plates with lettuce leaves and tomato slices. Top with salad.

Makes 4 to 6 servings

CAULIFLOWER CHOPPED SALAD

½ cup red wine vinegar

¼ cup olive oil

1 teaspoon salt

1 teaspoon honey

1 teaspoon Dijon mustard

½ teaspoon dried oregano

1 clove garlic, minced

¼ teaspoon black pepper

2 cups small cauliflower florets (½ inch)

1 head iceberg lettuce, chopped

1 container (4 ounces) crumbled blue cheese

1 pint grape tomatoes, halved *or* 1 cup finely chopped tomatoes

½ cup finely chopped red onion

2 green onions, finely chopped

1 avocado, diced

1. For cauliflower, whisk vinegar, oil, salt, honey, mustard, oregano, garlic and pepper in medium bowl. Add cauliflower; stir to coat. Cover and refrigerate several hours or overnight.

2. For salad, combine lettuce, blue cheese, tomatoes, red onion and green onions in large bowl; toss to coat.

3. Remove cauliflower from marinade using slotted spoon; place on salad. Whisk marinade; pour over salad and toss to coat. Top with avocado; mix gently.

Makes 8 servings

TIP

To make this recipe vegan, replace the honey with maple syrup and skip the cheese.

CHOPPED SALAD WITH CORN BREAD CROUTONS

½ **loaf corn bread (page 29)**

1 **large sweet potato, peeled and cut into 1-inch pieces**

5 **tablespoons olive oil, divided**

1½ **teaspoons salt, divided**

3 **tablespoons red wine vinegar**

2 **tablespoons white wine vinegar**

1 **tablespoon maple syrup**

1 **clove garlic, minced**

1 **teaspoon dry mustard**

⅛ **teaspoon dried oregano**

½ **cup vegetable oil**

1 **head iceberg lettuce, chopped**

1 **cup halved grape tomatoes**

2 **green onions, sliced**

1 **avocado, diced**

½ **cup chopped smoked almonds**

½ **cup dried cranberries**

1. Preheat oven to 400°F. Prepare corn bread. Cool in pan 10 minutes or cool completely; remove to cutting board. Cut half of corn bread into 1-inch cubes when cool enough to handle. Return to baking pan. *Reduce oven temperature to 350°F.* Bake 12 to 15 minutes or until corn bread cubes are dry and toasted, stirring once.

2. Spread sweet potato in 13×9-inch baking pan. Drizzle with 1 tablespoon olive oil and sprinkle with ½ teaspoon salt; toss to coat. Bake 30 to 35 minutes or until browned and tender, stirring once or twice. Cool completely.

3. For dressing, whisk red wine vinegar, white wine vinegar, maple syrup, garlic, mustard, oregano and remaining 1 teaspoon salt in medium bowl; whisk in remaining 4 tablespoons olive oil and vegetable oil in thin steady stream.

4. Combine lettuce, tomatoes, green onions and half of dressing in large bowl; mix well. Add sweet potato, avocado, almonds and cranberries; mix well. Taste and add additional dressing, if desired. Add croutons; mix gently.

Makes 6 to 8 servings

CORN BREAD

1¼ cups all-purpose flour

¾ cup yellow cornmeal

⅓ cup sugar

2 teaspoons baking powder

1 teaspoon salt

1¼ cups milk or oat milk

¼ cup (½ stick) butter or vegan plant butter, melted

1 egg or flax egg*

Stir 3 tablespoons boiling water into 1 tablespoon ground flaxseed in small bowl; cool completely.

1. Preheat oven to 400°F. Grease 8-inch square baking pan.

2. Combine flour, cornmeal, sugar, baking powder and salt in large bowl; mix well. Whisk milk, butter and egg in medium bowl until well blended. Add to flour mixture; stir just until dry ingredients are moistened. Pour batter into prepared baking pan.

3. Bake 25 minutes or until golden brown and toothpick inserted into center comes out clean.

KALE SALAD WITH CHERRIES AND AVOCADO

¼ **cup plus 1 teaspoon olive oil, divided**

3 **tablespoons uncooked quinoa**

¾ **teaspoon salt, divided**

3 **tablespoons balsamic vinegar**

1 **tablespoon red wine vinegar**

1 **tablespoon maple syrup**

2 **teaspoons Dijon mustard**

¼ **teaspoon dried oregano**

⅛ **teaspoon black pepper**

1 **large bunch kale (about 1 pound)**

1 **package (5 ounces) dried cherries**

2 **avocados, diced**

½ **cup smoked almonds, chopped**

1. Heat 1 teaspoon oil in small saucepan over medium-high heat. Add quinoa; cook and stir 3 to 5 minutes or until quinoa is golden brown and popped. Season with ¼ teaspoon salt. Remove to plate; cool completely.

2. Combine balsamic vinegar, red wine vinegar, maple syrup, mustard, oregano, pepper and remaining ½ teaspoon salt in medium bowl. Whisk in remaining ¼ cup oil until well blended.

3. Place kale in large bowl. Pour dressing over kale; massage dressing into leaves until well blended and kale is slightly softened. Add popped quinoa; stir until well blended. Add cherries, avocados and almonds; toss until blended.

Makes 6 to 8 servings

ROASTED BRUSSELS SPROUTS SALAD

BRUSSELS SPROUTS

- **1 pound brussels sprouts, trimmed and halved**
- **2 tablespoons olive oil**
- **½ teaspoon salt**

SALAD

- **2 cups coarsely chopped baby kale**
- **2 cups coarsely chopped romaine lettuce**
- **1½ cups candied pecans***
- **1 cup halved red grapes**
- **1 cup diced cucumbers**
- **½ cup dried cranberries**
- **½ cup fresh blueberries**
- **½ cup chopped red onion**
- **¼ cup toasted pepitas (pumpkin seeds)**
- **4 ounces crumbled goat cheese**

DRESSING

- **½ cup olive oil**
- **6 tablespoons balsamic vinegar**
- **6 tablespoons strawberry jam**
- **2 teaspoons Dijon mustard**
- **1 teaspoon salt**

*Candied or glazed pecans can be found in the produce section of the supermarket with other salad toppings, or they may be in the snack aisle.

1. For brussels sprouts, preheat oven to 400°F. Spray large baking sheet with nonstick cooking spray.

2. Combine brussels sprouts, 2 tablespoons oil and ½ teaspoon salt in medium bowl; toss to coat. Arrange brussels sprouts in single layer, cut sides down, on prepared baking sheet. Roast 20 minutes or until tender and browned, stirring once halfway through roasting. Cool completely on baking sheet.

3. For salad, combine kale, lettuce, pecans, grapes, cucumbers, cranberries, blueberries, red onion and pepitas in large bowl. Top with brussels sprouts and cheese.

4. For dressing, whisk ½ cup oil, vinegar, jam, mustard and
1 teaspoon salt in small bowl until well blended. Pour over salad; toss
gently to blend.

Makes 6 to 8 servings (about 8 cups)

Sandwiches

MEATLESS SLOPPY JOES

1 tablespoon olive oil

2 **cups thinly sliced onions**

2 **cups chopped green bell peppers**

2 **cloves garlic, minced**

2 **tablespoons ketchup**

1 **tablespoon yellow mustard**

1 **can (about 15 ounces) kidney beans, rinsed, drained and mashed**

1 **can (8 ounces) tomato sauce**

1 **teaspoon chili powder**

2 **tablespoons cider vinegar**

Salt and black pepper (optional)

4 **sandwich rolls**

1. Heat oil in large skillet over medium heat. Add onions, bell peppers and garlic; cook and stir 5 minutes or until vegetables are tender. Stir in ketchup and mustard.

2. Add beans, tomato sauce and chili powder. Reduce heat to medium-low. Cook 5 minutes or until thickened, stirring frequently. Stir in vinegar. Taste and season with salt and black pepper, if desired. Serve on sandwich rolls.

Makes 4 servings

TOMATO AND CHEESE MELTS

2 tablespoons mayonnaise

2 teaspoons prepared pesto

4 slices whole grain bread

4 tomato slices (about ¼ inch thick)

4 thin cucumber slices (⅛ inch thick and 3 inches long)

2 slices mozzarella cheese

1. Combine mayonnaise and pesto in small bowl; spread evenly on two bread slices. Top with tomato, cucumber, cheese and remaining bread slices.

2. Spray grill pan or large skillet with nonstick cooking spray; heat over medium heat. Cook sandwiches about 3 to 4 minutes per side or until lightly browned; reduce heat if toasting too quickly. Cover during last 2 minutes of cooking to melt cheese. Cut sandwiches in half.

Makes 2 servings

CHICKPEA SALAD

1 can (about 15 ounces) chickpeas, rinsed and drained

1 stalk celery, chopped

1 dill pickle, chopped (about ½ cup)

¼ cup finely chopped red or yellow onion

⅓ cup mayonnaise (regular or vegan)

1 teaspoon lemon juice

¼ teaspoon salt

Black pepper

Whole grain bread

Lettuce and tomato slices

1. Place chickpeas in medium bowl. Coarsely mash with potato masher, leaving some beans whole.

2. Add celery, pickle and onion; stir to mix. Add mayonnaise and lemon juice; mix well. Taste and add ¼ teaspoon salt or more, if desired. Season with pepper; mix well. Serve on bread with lettuce and tomato.

Makes 2 cups (4 to 6 servings)

GRILLED PORTOBELLO SANDWICHES

2 tablespoons olive oil, plus additional for brushing

1½ tablespoons balsamic vinegar

1 tablespoon Dijon mustard

1 tablespoon water

1 teaspoon dried oregano

1 clove garlic, minced

½ teaspoon black pepper

¼ teaspoon salt

4 large portobello mushroom caps, wiped with damp towel, gills and stems removed

8 slices multigrain Italian bread (8 ounces)

¼ cup crumbled blue cheese (optional)

2 ounces spring greens

1. Whisk 2 tablespoons oil, vinegar, mustard, water, oregano, garlic, pepper and salt in medium bowl until well blended. Place mushrooms in single layer on baking sheet or large plate. Brush 2 tablespoons dressing over mushrooms; set aside remaining dressing. Let mushrooms stand 30 minutes.

2. Spray grill pan with nonstick cooking spray; heat over medium-high heat. Brush both sides of bread with additional oil. Grill bread 1 minute per side, pressing down with spatula to flatten slightly. Set aside.

3. Grill mushrooms 3 to 4 minutes per side or until tender. Place each mushroom on one slice of bread. Sprinkle with blue cheese, if desired.

4. Whisk remaining dressing to blend. Add greens; stir to coat. Arrange spring greens on top of mushrooms; top with remaining bread slices.

Makes 4 servings

BARBECUE CAULIFLOWER CALZONES

1 **head cauliflower, cut into florets and thinly sliced**

2 **tablespoons olive oil**

Salt and black pepper

¾ **cup barbecue sauce**

1 **can (about 13 ounces) pizza dough**

½ **yellow onion, chopped**

1 **cup (4 ounces) shredded mozzarella cheese**

Ranch or blue cheese dressing

1. Preheat oven to 400°F.

2. Spread cauliflower on sheet pan; drizzle with oil and season lightly with salt and pepper. Toss to coat; spread in single layer.

3. Roast 30 minutes or until cauliflower is browned and very tender, stirring once. Transfer to medium bowl; stir in barbecue sauce.

4. Unroll pizza dough on cutting board. Stretch into 11×17-inch rectangle; cut into quarters. Place one fourth of onion on half of each piece of dough. Top with one fourth of cauliflower and ¼ cup cheese. Bring dough over filling; roll and pinch edges to seal. Place on baking sheet. Spray with nonstick cooking spray or brush with oil to help crust brown.

5. Bake 10 minutes or until golden brown. Serve with ranch dressing.

Makes 4 servings

MUSHROOM TOFU BURGERS

7 ounces extra firm tofu, crumbled

3 teaspoons olive oil, divided

1 package (8 ounces) cremini mushrooms, coarsely chopped

½ medium onion, coarsely chopped

1 clove garlic, minced

1 cup old-fashioned oats

⅓ cup finely chopped walnuts

1 egg

½ teaspoon salt

½ teaspoon onion powder

¼ teaspoon dried thyme

6 English muffins, split and toasted

Lettuce, tomato and red onion slices (optional)

1. Place tofu on small baking sheet. Freeze 1 hour or until firm.

2. Heat 1 teaspoon oil in large nonstick skillet over medium heat. Add mushrooms, onion and garlic; cook and stir 10 minutes or until mushrooms have released most of their liquid. Remove from heat; cool slightly.

3. Combine mushroom mixture, tofu, oats, walnuts, egg, salt, onion powder and thyme in food processor or blender; process until combined. (Some larger tofu pieces may remain). Shape mixture by ⅓-cupfuls into six patties.

4. Heat 1 teaspoon oil in same skillet over medium-low heat. Working in batches, cook patties 5 minutes per side or until browned, adding remaining 1 teaspoon oil between batches.

5. Serve burgers on English muffins with lettuce, tomato and red onion, if desired.

Makes 6 servings

GRILLED GARDEN BRUSCHETTA

1 medium zucchini, cut into ¼-inch diagonal slices

1 large shallot or small red onion, thinly sliced

1 teaspoon olive oil

¼ teaspoon black pepper

4 slices artisan whole wheat bread

2 cloves garlic, crushed

2 plum tomatoes, thinly sliced

¼ teaspoon dried oregano

2 tablespoons chopped fresh basil

4 jumbo pimiento-stuffed olives, thinly sliced

4 tablespoons shredded Parmesan cheese

1. Preheat grill to medium-high heat. Place zucchini and shallot slices in grill basket or vegetable grate. Brush with oil and sprinkle with pepper. Grill 3 to 5 minutes per side, or until tender and lightly browned.* Remove from heat.

2. Rub bread slices with garlic; discard garlic. Grill bread 1 to 2 minutes or until lightly browned.**

3. Arrange tomato slices on each bread slice; sprinkle with oregano and basil. Top with zucchini and shallot. Arrange sliced olives over vegetables. Sprinkle cheese on each serving.

4. Place bruschetta on grill rack or vegetable grate; grill 2 minutes or until cheese is melted and bruschetta is hot.***

Makes 2 servings

*Or cook vegetables in 1 teaspoon oil in large skillet over medium-high heat until tender.
**Or toast bread slices under broiler 20 seconds or until browned.
***Or place on baking sheet and broil 20 to 30 seconds until cheese melts.*

FARRO VEGGIE BURGERS

1½ **cups water**

½ **cup pearled farro**

2 **medium potatoes, peeled and quartered**

2 **to 4 tablespoons canola oil, divided**

¾ **cup finely chopped green onions**

1 **cup grated carrots**

2 **teaspoons grated fresh ginger**

2 **tablespoons ground almonds (almond meal)**

¾ **teaspoon salt**

¼ **teaspoon black pepper**

½ **cup panko bread crumbs**

6 **whole wheat hamburger buns**

Ketchup and mustard (optional)

1. Combine 1½ cups water and farro in medium saucepan; bring to a boil over high heat. Reduce heat to low; partially cover and cook 25 to 30 minutes or until farro is tender. Drain and cool.

2. Meanwhile, place potatoes in large saucepan; cover with water. Bring to a boil; reduce heat and simmer 20 minutes or until tender. Cool and mash potatoes; set aside.

3. Heat 1 tablespoon oil in medium skillet over medium-high heat. Add green onions; cook and stir 1 minute. Add carrots and ginger; cover and cook 2 to 3 minutes or until carrots are tender. Transfer to large bowl; cool completely.

4. Add mashed potatoes and farro to carrot mixture. Add almonds, salt and pepper; mix well. Shape mixture into six patties. Spread panko on medium plate; coat patties with panko.

5. Heat 1 tablespoon oil in large nonstick skillet over medium heat. Cook patties about 4 minutes per side or until golden brown, adding additional oil as needed. Serve on buns with desired condiments.

Makes 6 servings

MEDITERRANEAN ROASTED VEGETABLE WRAPS

1 head cauliflower, cut into 1-inch florets

4 tablespoons olive oil, divided

2 teaspoons ras el hanout, 7-spice blend, shawarma blend or za'atar

1 teaspoon salt, divided

1 zucchini, quartered lengthwise and cut into ¼-inch pieces

1 yellow squash, quartered lengthwise and cut into ¼-inch pieces

½ red onion, thinly sliced

¼ cup red pepper sauce (avjar)

4 large thin pitas or lavash (10 inches)

4 ounces feta cheese, crumbled

1 cup cooked chickpeas

¼ cup diced tomatoes

¼ cup minced fresh parsley

¼ cup diced cucumber (optional)

2 teaspoons vegetable oil

1. Preheat oven to 400°F. Combine cauliflower, 2 tablespoons olive oil, ras el hanout and ½ teaspoon salt in large bowl; toss to coat. Spread on half of sheet pan. Combine zucchini, yellow squash, onion, remaining 2 tablespoons olive oil and ½ teaspoon salt in same bowl; toss to coat. Spread on other side of sheet pan. Roast 25 minutes or until vegetables are browned and tender, stirring once. Cool slightly.

2. Spread 1 tablespoon red pepper sauce on one pita. Top with one fourth of vegetables, feta, chickpeas, tomatoes, parsley and cucumber, if desired. Fold two sides over filling; roll up into burrito shape. Repeat with remaining ingredients.

3. Heat 1 teaspoon vegetable oil in large skillet over medium-high heat. Add two wraps, seam sides down; cook 1 minute or until browned. Turn and cook other side until browned. Repeat with remaining vegetable oil and wraps. Cut in half to serve.

Makes 4 servings

Main Dishes

MEXICAN CAULIFLOWER AND BEAN SKILLET

1 teaspoon olive oil

3 cups coarsely chopped cauliflower

¾ teaspoon salt

½ medium yellow onion, chopped

1 green bell pepper, chopped

1 clove garlic, minced

1 teaspoon chili powder

¾ teaspoon ground cumin

Dash ground red pepper

1 can (about 15 ounces) black beans, rinsed and drained

1 cup (4 ounces) shredded Cheddar-Jack cheese

Salsa and sour cream

1. Heat oil in large cast iron skillet over medium-high heat. Add cauliflower and salt; cook and stir 5 minutes. Add onion, bell pepper, garlic, chili powder, cumin and ground red pepper; cook and stir 5 minutes or until cauliflower is tender. Add beans; cook until beans are heated through. Remove from heat.

2. Sprinkle with cheese; fold gently and let stand until melted. Serve with salsa and sour cream.

Makes 4 to 6 servings

LEEK AND CHIVE CHAMP

3 medium russet potatoes (1½ pounds), peeled and cut into 1-inch pieces

6 tablespoons butter or vegan plant butter, divided

2 large leeks, halved and sliced

½ cup milk or oat milk

¼ cup chopped fresh chives

½ teaspoon salt

¼ teaspoon black pepper

½ cup prepared French fried onions

1. Place potatoes in large saucepan; add cold water to cover by 2 inches. Bring to a boil over medium-high heat; cook 16 to 18 minutes or until tender. Drain and return to saucepan.

2. Meanwhile, melt 2 tablespoons butter in medium skillet over medium heat. Add leeks; cook 5 to 6 minutes or until tender, stirring occasionally.

3. Heat milk in small saucepan over medium-high heat until hot. Add 2 tablespoons butter; cook until melted. Pour milk mixture into saucepan with potatoes; mash until smooth. Stir in leeks, chives, salt and pepper; mix well.

4. Spoon into serving bowl; make large indentation in top of potatoes. Melt remaining 2 tablespoons butter; pour into indentation. Sprinkle with fried onions.

Makes 4 to 6 servings

CORNMEAL-CRUSTED CAULIFLOWER STEAKS

½ **cup cornmeal**

¼ **cup all-purpose flour**

1 **teaspoon salt**

1 **teaspoon dried sage**

½ **teaspoon garlic powder**

Black pepper

½ **cup milk or oat milk**

2 **heads cauliflower**

4 **tablespoons butter or vegan plant butter, melted**

Barbecue sauce (optional)

1. Preheat oven to 400°F. Line baking sheet with parchment paper.

2. Combine cornmeal, flour, salt, sage and garlic powder in shallow bowl or baking pan. Season with pepper. Pour milk into another shallow bowl.

3. Turn cauliflower stem side up on cutting board. Trim away leaves, leaving stem intact. Slice through stem into 2 or 3 slices. Trim off excess florets from two end slices, creating flat "steaks." Repeat with remaining cauliflower; reserve extra cauliflower for another use.

4. Dip cauliflower into milk to coat both sides. Place in cornmeal mixture; pat onto all sides of cauliflower. Place on prepared baking sheet. Drizzle butter evenly over cauliflower.

5. Bake 40 minutes or until cauliflower is tender. Serve with barbecue sauce for dipping, if desired.

Makes 4 servings

SESAME NOODLE BOWL

1 **package (16 ounces) uncooked spaghetti**

6 **tablespoons soy sauce**

5 **tablespoons dark sesame oil**

3 **tablespoons sugar**

3 **tablespoons rice vinegar**

4 **tablespoons vegetable oil, divided**

3 **cloves garlic, minced**

1 **teaspoon grated fresh ginger or ginger paste**

½ **teaspoon sriracha sauce**

2 **green onions, sliced**

1 **red bell pepper**

1 **cucumber**

1 **carrot**

1 **package (14 to 16 ounces) firm tofu, drained and patted dry**

Sesame seeds

1. Cook spaghetti in large saucepan of salted boiling water according to package directions for al dente. Drain, reserving 1 tablespoon water.

2. Whisk soy sauce, sesame oil, sugar, vinegar, 2 tablespoons vegetable oil, garlic, ginger and sriracha in large bowl. Stir in noodles, reserved pasta cooking water and green onions. Let stand at least 30 minutes or until noodles have cooled to room temperature and most of sauce is absorbed, stirring occasionally.

3. Meanwhile, cut bell pepper into thin strips. Peel cucumber and carrot and shred with julienne peeler into long strands, or cut into thin strips.

4. Cut tofu into thin triangles or 1-inch cubes. Heat remaining 2 tablespoons vegetable oil in large nonstick skillet over high heat. Add tofu; cook 5 minutes or until browned on both sides, turning occasionally.

5. Place noodles in bowls. Top with tofu, bell pepper, cucumber and carrot. Sprinkle with sesame seeds.

Makes 6 servings

TIP

Sesame noodles are great served warm or cold. To serve them cold, cover and refrigerate a few hours or overnight after step 2 before preparing the vegetables and tofu. For a side dish or potluck dish, skip the tofu and stir the vegetables into the noodles after they are cool. Refrigerate until ready to serve.

TOFU AND SWEET POTATO BOWL

1 **package (14 to 16 ounces) firm tofu, drained**

1 **cup plus 4 tablespoons water, divided**

2 **teaspoons salt**

1½ **teaspoons sugar**

2 **tablespoons plus 2 teaspoons soy sauce, divided**

1 **tablespoon plus 1 teaspoon dark sesame oil, divided**

2 **sweet potatoes, peeled, if desired**

2 **tablespoons vegetable oil**

3 **tablespoons tahini**

1 **tablespoon peanut butter**

2 **teaspoons rice vinegar**

1 **teaspoon maple syrup**

Dash ground red pepper

Hot cooked brown rice

1 **avocado, sliced**

Chopped mixed greens and sprouts

Black sesame seeds

1. Place tofu on cutting board on one long narrow side. Cut into thirds. Turn tofu onto wide side; cut in half lengthwise and crosswise forming 12 pieces. Place in 9-inch baking dish.

2. Heat 1 cup water, salt and sugar in small saucepan over medium heat until salt and sugar have dissolved. Whisk in 2 tablespoons soy sauce and 1 tablespoon sesame oil. Pour over tofu; let stand at least 30 minutes.

3. Cut sweet potatoes in half lengthwise; cut crosswise into ¼-inch slices. Bring large saucepan of salted water to a boil. Add sweet potatoes; cook 12 to 15 minutes or until fork-tender. Drain.

4. Drain tofu and pat dry. Heat vegetable oil in large nonstick skillet over medium-high heat. Add tofu in single layer; cook 5 minutes or until browned on bottoms. Turn tofu and cook 5 minutes or until other sides are browned.

5. For sauce, whisk tahini, peanut butter, rice vinegar, maple syrup, red pepper, remaining 2 teaspoons soy sauce and 1 teaspoon sesame oil in medium bowl. Whisk in remaining 4 tablespoons water, one at a time, until mixture is smooth and desired consistency.

6. Divide rice, sweet potatoes, tofu and avocado among four bowls. Add chopped greens and sprouts. Serve with sauce; garnish with sesame seeds.

Makes 4 servings

SOBA TERIYAKI BOWL

¾ cup plus
1 tablespoon
cornstarch,
divided

2 teaspoons salt,
divided

½ cup plus
2 tablespoons
water, divided

1 head cauliflower,
cut into 1-inch
florets

¾ cup pineapple
juice

¾ cup soy sauce

2 tablespoons
packed brown
sugar

1 tablespoon lime
juice

1 teaspoon minced
garlic

6 ounces uncooked
soba noodles

5 cups shredded
red, green or
mixed cabbage
or 1 package
(14 ounces)
coleslaw mix

½ cup unseasoned
rice vinegar

1 teaspoon
granulated sugar

Chopped green
onions and
sesame seeds

1. Preheat oven to 400°F. Spray large baking sheet with nonstick cooking spray. Whisk ¾ cup cornstarch and 1 teaspoon salt in medium bowl. Whisk in ½ cup water until smooth. Dip cauliflower into mixture; place in single layer on prepared baking sheet. Bake 20 minutes or until tender.

2. Meanwhile, bring pineapple juice, soy sauce, brown sugar, lime juice and garlic to a simmer in small saucepan. Whisk remaining 2 tablespoons water into remaining 1 tablespoon cornstarch in small bowl; stir into sauce. Reduce heat to low; cook and stir 5 minutes. Transfer to large bowl; cool slightly. Remove ¼ cup sauce; set aside.

3. Cook soba noodles according to package directions. Drain and rinse under cold water until cool. Divide among serving bowls.

4. Combine cabbage, vinegar, granulated sugar and remaining 1 teaspoon salt in medium bowl; mix and squeeze with hands until well blended.

5. Add cauliflower to large bowl of sauce; stir to coat. Divide among serving bowls. Drizzle some of reserved sauce over noodles. Serve with cabbage mixture. Sprinkle with green onions and sesame seeds.

Makes 4 servings

LENTIL BOLOGNESE

2 tablespoons olive oil

1 onion, chopped

1 carrot, chopped

1 stalk celery, chopped

2 cloves garlic, minced

1 teaspoon salt

½ teaspoon dried oregano

Pinch red pepper flakes

3 tablespoons tomato paste

¼ cup dry white wine

1 can (28 ounces) crushed tomatoes

1 can (about 14 ounces) diced tomatoes

1 cup dried lentils, rinsed

1 portobello mushroom, gills removed, finely chopped

1½ cups water or vegetable broth

Hot cooked pasta

1. Heat oil in large saucepan over medium heat. Add onion, carrot and celery; cook and stir 10 minutes or until onion is lightly browned and carrot is softened.

2. Stir in garlic, salt, oregano and red pepper flakes. Add tomato paste; cook and stir 1 minute. Add wine; cook and stir until absorbed. Stir in crushed tomatoes, diced tomatoes, lentils, mushroom and water; bring to a simmer.

3. Reduce heat to medium; partially cover and cook about 40 minutes or until lentils are tender, removing cover after 20 minutes. Serve over pasta.

Makes 6 to 8 servings

LEMON CREAM PASTA WITH ROASTED CAULIFLOWER

1 large head cauliflower *or* 2 heads broccoli (2½ pounds), cut into 1-inch florets

2 tablespoons olive oil

1 teaspoon salt, divided

¼ teaspoon plus ⅛ teaspoon black pepper, divided

8 ounces uncooked cavatappi pasta

¼ cup (½ stick) butter, cut into pieces

¼ cup all-purpose flour

2 cups milk

½ cup shredded Parmesan cheese

Grated peel and juice of 1 lemon

¼ cup chopped almonds

Baby arugula

Aleppo pepper or red pepper flakes (optional)

1. Preheat oven to 425°F. Place cauliflower on large baking sheet. Drizzle with oil and sprinkle with ½ teaspoon salt and ¼ teaspoon black pepper; toss to coat. Roast about 30 minutes or until cauliflower is well browned and tender.

2. Cook pasta in large saucepan of salted boiling water according to package directions for al dente. Drain, reserving 1 cup pasta cooking water. Place pasta in large bowl; add cauliflower.

3. Melt butter in same saucepan over medium heat; whisk in flour until smooth paste forms. Whisk in milk, remaining ½ teaspoon salt and ⅛ teaspoon black pepper; cook 2 to 3 minutes or until thickened. Whisk in ½ cup reserved pasta water and Parmesan until smooth. Pour over pasta and cauliflower; stir to coat. Add additional pasta water by tablespoonfuls to loosen sauce, if needed. Stir in lemon juice and almonds. Top with arugula or gently fold into pasta mixture. Sprinkle with lemon peel and Aleppo pepper, if desired.

Makes 6 to 8 servings

PEANUT BUTTER TOFU BOWL

¼ cup peanut butter

¼ cup hoisin sauce

1 tablespoon packed brown sugar

1 tablespoon dark sesame oil

1 tablespoon water

1½ teaspoons minced fresh ginger

1½ tablespoons rice vinegar, divided

1½ tablespoons soy sauce, divided

2 cloves garlic, minced, divided

½ teaspoon sriracha sauce

1 package (14 to 16 ounces) firm tofu, cut into 1-inch cubes

¼ cup cornstarch

2 tablespoons plus 1 teaspoon vegetable oil, divided

1 head bok choy

Hot cooked rice

Chopped peanuts and/or minced fresh cilantro (optional)

1. For sauce, combine peanut butter, hoisin, brown sugar, sesame oil, 1 tablespoon water, ginger, 1½ teaspoons vinegar, 1½ teaspoons soy sauce, 1 clove garlic and sriracha in small saucepan. Cook over medium-low heat 5 minutes, whisking frequently.

2. Toss tofu with cornstarch in large bowl. Heat 2 tablespoons vegetable oil in large nonstick skillet over high heat. Add tofu to skillet; cook without stirring 5 minutes or until well browned and crusted on bottom. Turn and cook 5 minutes or until browned on other side. Cook 2 minutes, turning frequently until other sides of tofu are lightly browned. Add sauce; cook 1 minute or until tofu is glazed.

3. Meanwhile, separate leaves and stems of bok choy. Coarsely chop stems and leaves separately. Heat remaining 1 teaspoon vegetable oil in medium skillet over medium-high heat. Add bok choy stems; cook and stir 3 minutes. Add leaves and remaining 1 clove garlic; cook and stir 1 minute. Add remaining 1 tablespoon soy sauce and 1 tablespoon vinegar; cook and stir 30 seconds.

4. Divide tofu, bok choy and rice among bowls. Garnish with peanuts.

Makes 4 servings

CHICKPEA TIKKA MASALA

1 tablespoon olive oil

1 onion, chopped

3 cloves garlic, minced

1 tablespoon minced fresh ginger or ginger paste

1 tablespoon garam masala

1 teaspoon ground cumin

1 teaspoon ground coriander

1 teaspoon salt

¼ teaspoon ground red pepper

2 cans (about 15 ounces each) chickpeas, rinsed and drained

1 can (28 ounces) crushed tomatoes

1 can (about 13 ounces) coconut milk

1 package (about 12 ounces) firm silken tofu, drained and cut into 1-inch cubes

Hot cooked brown basmati rice

Chopped fresh cilantro

1. Heat oil in large saucepan over medium-high heat. Add onion; cook and stir 5 minutes or until translucent. Add garlic, ginger, garam masala, cumin, coriander, salt and red pepper; cook and stir 1 minute. Stir in chickpeas, tomatoes and coconut milk.

2. Reduce heat to medium; simmer 30 minutes or until sauce has thickened and chickpeas have softened slightly.

3. Add tofu; stir gently. Cook 7 to 10 minutes or until tofu is heated through. Serve over rice; garnish with cilantro.

Makes 4 servings

SWEET POTATO MAKI BOWL

2 tablespoons vegetable oil, divided

1 large sweet potato (18 to 20 ounces), peeled

½ cup panko bread crumbs

½ teaspoon salt, divided

⅛ teaspoon ground red pepper

⅓ cup water

¼ cup cornstarch

1 cup Calrose rice, sushi rice or other short grain rice

1 tablespoon rice vinegar

1 teaspoon granulated sugar

½ cup soy sauce

1 tablespoon packed brown sugar

¼ cup mayonnaise

1 tablespoon sriracha sauce

½ cucumber, cut in half lengthwise and thinly sliced

1 avocado, diced

Sesame seeds

1. Preheat oven to 400°F. Line large baking sheet with foil; brush with 1 tablespoon oil.

2. Cut sweet potato in half lengthwise; cut crosswise into ¼-inch slices. Combine panko, ¼ teaspoon salt and red pepper in shallow bowl. Combine ⅓ cup water, cornstarch and remaining ¼ teaspoon salt in another shallow bowl; mix until smooth. Dip sweet potato slices in cornstarch mixture, letting excess drip back into bowl. Roll in panko mixture to coat; place on prepared baking sheet.

3. Bake 20 to 25 minutes or until potatoes are tender and coating is golden brown, turning once.

4. Meanwhile, cook rice according to package directions. Stir vinegar and granulated sugar into cooked rice.

5. Combine soy sauce and brown sugar in small saucepan; cook over low heat until mixture is reduced and syrupy. Combine mayonnaise and sriracha in small bowl.

6. For each serving, place rice in bowls. Top with sweet potatoes, cucumber and avocado; drizzle with soy sauce mixture and sprinkle with sesame seeds. Serve with sriracha mayonnaise.

Makes 4 servings

Vegetables

CREAMY SLAB POTATOES

¼ **cup (½ stick) butter, melted**

1 **teaspoon salt**

½ **teaspoon dried rosemary**

½ **teaspoon dried thyme**

¼ **teaspoon black pepper**

2½ **pounds Yukon Gold potatoes, peeled and cut crosswise into 1-inch slices (6 to 8 potatoes)**

1 **cup water**

3 **cloves garlic, smashed**

1. Preheat oven to 500°F.

2. Combine butter, salt, rosemary, thyme and pepper in 13×9-inch baking pan (do not use glass); mix well. Add potatoes; toss to coat. Spread in single layer.

3. Bake 15 minutes. Turn potatoes; bake 15 minutes. Add water and garlic to pan; bake 15 minutes. Remove to serving plate; pour any remaining liquid in pan over potatoes.

Makes 4 servings

BALSAMIC BUTTERNUT SQUASH

3 tablespoons olive oil

2 tablespoons thinly sliced fresh sage (about 6 large leaves), divided

1 medium butternut squash, peeled and cut into 1-inch pieces (4 to 5 cups)

½ red onion, halved and cut into ¼-inch slices

1 teaspoon salt, divided

2½ tablespoons balsamic vinegar

¼ teaspoon black pepper

1. Heat oil in large (12-inch) cast iron skillet over medium-high heat. Add 1 tablespoon sage; cook and stir 3 minutes. Add squash, onion and ½ teaspoon salt; cook 6 minutes, stirring occasionally. Reduce heat to medium; cook 15 minutes without stirring.

2. Stir in vinegar, remaining ½ teaspoon salt and pepper; cook 10 minutes or until squash is tender, stirring occasionally. Stir in remaining 1 tablespoon sage; cook 1 minute.

Makes 4 servings

CRISPY SMASHED POTATOES

1 **tablespoon plus ½ teaspoon salt, divided**

3 **pounds unpeeled small red potatoes (2 inches or smaller)**

4 **tablespoons butter, melted, or olive oil, divided**

¼ **teaspoon black pepper**

½ **cup grated Parmesan cheese (optional)**

1. Fill large saucepan with water; add 1 tablespoon salt. Bring to a boil over high heat. Add potatoes; boil about 20 minutes or until potatoes are tender when pierced with tip of sharp knife. Drain potatoes; set aside until cool enough to handle.

2. Preheat oven to 450°F. Brush baking sheet with 2 tablespoons butter. Working with one potato at a time, smash with hand or bottom of measuring cup to about ½-inch thickness. Arrange smashed potatoes in single layer on prepared baking sheet. Brush with remaining 2 tablespoons butter; sprinkle with remaining ½ teaspoon salt and pepper.

3. Bake 30 to 40 minutes or until bottoms of potatoes are golden brown. Turn potatoes; bake 10 minutes. Sprinkle with cheese, if desired; bake 5 minutes or until cheese is melted.

Makes about 6 servings

CREAMY COLESLAW

½ **cup mayonnaise**

½ **cup buttermilk**

2 **teaspoons sugar**

1 **teaspoon celery seed**

1 **teaspoon lime juice**

½ **teaspoon chili powder**

3 **cups shredded coleslaw mix**

1 **cup shredded carrots**

¼ **cup finely chopped red onion**

1. Whisk mayonnaise, buttermilk, sugar, celery seed, lime juice and chili powder in large bowl until smooth and well blended. Add coleslaw mix, carrots and onion; toss to coat evenly.

2. Cover and refrigerate at least 2 hours before serving.

Makes 4 servings

POTATO CAKES WITH BRUSSELS SPROUTS

2½ **pounds Yukon Gold potatoes, peeled and cut into 1-inch cubes**

6 **tablespoons butter, melted**

⅓ **cup milk, warmed**

2 **teaspoons salt**

½ **teaspoon black pepper**

3 **tablespoons vegetable oil, divided**

12 **ounces brussels sprouts, ends trimmed, thinly sliced**

4 **green onions, thinly sliced on the diagonal**

1. Place potatoes in large saucepan or Dutch oven; add cold water to cover by 2 inches. Bring to a boil over high heat. Reduce heat to medium-low; cover and simmer about 10 minutes or until potatoes are tender. Drain.

2. Return potatoes to saucepan; mash with potato masher until slightly chunky. Stir in butter, milk, salt and pepper until well blended; set aside.

3. Heat 1 tablespoon oil in large nonstick skillet over medium-high heat. Add brussels sprouts; cook about 8 minutes or until tender and lightly browned, stirring occasionally. Stir brussels sprouts and green onions into potato mixture. Wipe out skillet with paper towel.

4. Heat 1 tablespoon oil in skillet over medium heat. Drop potato mixture into skillet by ½ cupfuls, spacing about ½ inch apart. Cook about 3 minutes per side or until cakes are browned and crisp, pressing down lightly with spatula. Transfer to platter; tent with foil to keep warm. Repeat with remaining 1 tablespoon oil and potato mixture.

Makes 12 cakes

SWEET POTATO AND APPLE CASSEROLE

1 cup all-purpose flour

¾ cup (1½ sticks) butter, melted, divided

½ cup packed brown sugar

¾ teaspoon salt, divided

½ teaspoon ground cinnamon

¼ teaspoon ground nutmeg or mace

¼ teaspoon ground cardamom

2 pounds sweet potatoes, peeled, halved lengthwise and thinly sliced

2 Granny Smith apples, peeled, cored, halved lengthwise and thinly sliced

1. Preheat oven to 375°F. Spray 2-quart baking dish with nonstick cooking spray.

2. Combine flour, ½ cup butter, brown sugar, ½ teaspoon salt, cinnamon, nutmeg and cardamom in medium bowl until well blended.

3. Arrange sweet potatoes and apples in prepared baking dish. Drizzle with remaining ¼ cup butter; sprinkle with remaining ¼ teaspoon salt.

4. Crumble topping over sweet potatoes and apples. Bake 35 to 40 minutes or until topping is brown and potatoes and apples are tender.

Makes 8 servings

CORN FRITTERS

2 large ears corn

2 eggs, separated

¼ cup all-purpose flour

1 tablespoon sugar

1 tablespoon butter, melted

¼ teaspoon salt

⅛ teaspoon black pepper

⅛ teaspoon cream of tartar

1 to 2 tablespoons vegetable oil

1. Husk corn. Cut kernels from ears (1½ to 2 cups); place in medium bowl. Hold cobs over bowl; scrape with back of knife to extract juice. Transfer about half of kernels to food processor; process 2 to 3 seconds or until coarsely chopped. Add to whole kernels.

2. Whisk egg yolks in large bowl. Whisk in flour, sugar, butter, salt and pepper. Stir in corn mixture.

3. Beat egg whites and cream of tartar in separate large bowl with electric mixer at high speed until stiff peaks form. Fold egg whites into corn mixture.

4. Heat 1 tablespoon oil in large nonstick skillet over medium-high heat. Drop ¼ cupfuls of batter 1 inch apart into skillet. Cook 3 to 5 minutes per side or until lightly browned. Repeat with remaining batter, adding more oil, if necessary. Serve hot.

Makes 8 to 9 fritters

GREEN BEAN POTATO SALAD

½ cup thinly sliced red onion

¼ cup plus 2 tablespoons white wine vinegar, divided

2 tablespoons water

1 teaspoon sugar

1½ teaspoons salt, divided

2 cups cubed assorted potatoes (purple, baby red, Yukon Gold and/or a combination)

1 cup cut fresh green beans (1-inch pieces)

2 tablespoons plain Greek yogurt

2 tablespoons olive oil

1 tablespoon spicy brown mustard

1. Combine onion, ¼ cup vinegar, 2 tablespoons water, sugar and ½ teaspoon salt in large glass jar. Seal jar; shake well. Refrigerate at least 1 hour or up to 1 week.

2. Bring large saucepan of water to a boil. Add potatoes; cook 5 to 8 minutes or until fork-tender. Drain and return to saucepan to cool.

3. Meanwhile, bring medium saucepan of water to a boil. Add green beans; cook 4 minutes. Drain and run under cold water to stop cooking.

4. Whisk yogurt, oil, mustard, remaining 2 tablespoons vinegar and 1 teaspoon salt in large bowl until smooth and well blended.

5. Add potatoes and green beans to dressing. Drain onions; add to bowl with potatoes. Toss gently to coat. Cover and refrigerate at least 1 hour before serving to allow flavors to develop.

Makes 6 servings

BRUSSELS SPROUTS WITH CARAMELIZED ONIONS

1 **pound brussels sprouts, trimmed and halved lengthwise**

1 **tablespoon vegetable or olive oil**

1 **cup chopped onion**

2 **tablespoons molasses or maple syrup, divided**

1 **tablespoon balsamic vinegar**

3 **tablespoons dry white wine, divided**

Salt and black pepper

1. Bring medium saucepan of water to a boil. Add brussels sprouts; cook 5 minutes. Drain.

2. Heat oil in large skillet over medium-low heat. Add onion; cook and stir 10 minutes or until tender and lightly browned. Add 1 tablespoon molasses and vinegar; cook 5 minutes.

3. Add brussels sprouts to skillet with onion and increase heat to medium. Add 2 tablespoons wine and remaining 1 tablespoon molasses; cook about 3 minutes or until most liquid has evaporated.

4. Add remaining 1 tablespoon wine to skillet; cook and stir 2 minutes or until brussels sprouts are tender. Season with salt and pepper.

Makes 4 servings

BOXTY PANCAKES

2 **medium russet potatoes (1 pound), peeled, divided**

⅔ **cup all-purpose flour**

1 **teaspoon baking powder**

½ **teaspoon salt**

⅔ **cup buttermilk**

3 **tablespoons butter**

1. Cut one potato into 1-inch chunks; place in small saucepan and add cold water to cover by 2 inches. Bring to a boil over medium-high heat; cook 14 to 18 minutes or until tender. Drain potato; return to saucepan and mash. Transfer to medium bowl.

2. Grate remaining potato on large holes of box grater; add to bowl with mashed potato. Stir in flour, baking powder and salt until blended. Stir in buttermilk.

3. Melt 1 tablespoon butter in large nonstick skillet over medium heat. Drop four slightly heaping tablespoonfuls of batter into skillet; flatten into 2½-inch circles. Cook about 4 minutes per side or until golden and puffed. Remove to plate; cover to keep warm. Repeat with remaining batter and butter. Serve immediately.

Makes 4 servings (16 to 20 pancakes)

TIP

Serve with melted butter, sour cream or maple syrup.

Soups & Chilis

BLACK BEAN SOUP

2 tablespoons
   vegetable oil

1 cup diced onion

1 stalk celery, diced

2 carrots, diced

½ small green bell
   pepper, diced

4 cloves garlic,
   minced

4 cans (about
   15 ounces each)
   black beans,
   rinsed and
   drained, divided

4 cups (32 ounces)
   vegetable broth,
   divided

2 tablespoons cider
   vinegar

2 teaspoons chili
   powder

½ teaspoon salt

½ teaspoon ground
   red pepper

½ teaspoon ground
   cumin

¼ teaspoon liquid
   smoke

   Optional toppings:
   sour cream,
   chopped
   green onions
   and shredded
   Cheddar cheese

1. Heat oil in large saucepan or Dutch oven over medium-low heat. Add onion, celery, carrots, bell pepper and garlic; cook 10 minutes, stirring occasionally.

2. Combine half of beans and 1 cup broth in food processor or blender; process until smooth. Add to vegetables in saucepan.

3. Stir in remaining beans, remaining broth, vinegar, chili powder, salt, red pepper, cumin and liquid smoke; bring to a boil over high heat. Reduce heat to medium-low; simmer 1 hour or until vegetables are tender and soup is thickened.

4. Ladle into bowls. Serve with desired toppings.

Makes 4 to 6 servings

CREAMY TOMATO SOUP

3 tablespoons olive oil, divided

2 tablespoons butter

1 large onion, finely chopped

2 cloves garlic, minced

2 teaspoons sugar

1 teaspoon salt

½ teaspoon dried oregano

2 cans (28 ounces each) peeled Italian plum tomatoes, undrained

4 cups ½-inch focaccia cubes (half of 9-ounce loaf)

½ teaspoon black pepper

½ cup whipping cream

1. Heat 2 tablespoons oil and butter in large saucepan over medium-high heat. Add onion; cook and stir 5 minutes or until softened. Add garlic, sugar, salt and oregano; cook 30 seconds. Stir in tomatoes with juice; bring to a boil. Reduce heat to medium-low; simmer 45 minutes, stirring occasionally.

2. Meanwhile, prepare croutons. Preheat oven to 350°F. Combine focaccia cubes, remaining 1 tablespoon oil and pepper in large bowl; toss to coat. Spread on large baking sheet. Bake about 10 minutes or until bread cubes are golden brown.

3. Blend soup with immersion blender until smooth. (Or process in batches in food processor or blender.) Stir in cream; heat through. Serve soup topped with croutons.

Makes 4 servings

WEST AFRICAN PEANUT SOUP

2 tablespoons
vegetable oil

1 large onion,
chopped

½ cup chopped
roasted peanuts

1½ tablespoons
minced fresh
ginger

4 cloves garlic,
minced

1 teaspoon salt

4 cups vegetable
broth

2 sweet potatoes,
peeled and
cut into ½-inch
cubes

1 can (28 ounces)
whole tomatoes,
drained and
coarsely
chopped

¼ teaspoon ground
red pepper

1 bunch Swiss chard
or kale, stemmed
and thinly sliced

⅓ cup unsweetened
peanut butter
(creamy or
chunky)

1. Heat oil in large saucepan over medium-high heat. Add onion; cook and stir 5 minutes or until softened. Add peanuts, ginger, garlic and salt; cook and stir 1 minute. Stir in broth, sweet potatoes, tomatoes and red pepper; bring to a boil. Reduce heat to medium; simmer 10 minutes.

2. Stir in Swiss chard and peanut butter; cook over medium-low heat 10 minutes or until vegetables are tender and soup is creamy.

Makes 6 to 8 servings

QUINOA CHILI

2 tablespoons vegetable oil

1 onion, chopped

1 red bell pepper, chopped

1 large carrot, diced

1 stalk celery, diced

1 jalapeño pepper, seeded and finely chopped

1 tablespoon minced garlic

3 tablespoons chili powder

2 teaspoons ground cumin

1 teaspoon salt

1 can (28 ounces) crushed tomatoes

1 can (about 15 ounces) kidney beans, rinsed and drained

1 cup water

1 cup corn

½ cup uncooked quinoa, rinsed well in fine-mesh strainer

Optional toppings: diced avocado, shredded Cheddar cheese and sliced green onions

1. Heat oil in large saucepan over medium-high heat. Add onion, bell pepper, carrot and celery; cook about 10 minutes or until vegetables are softened, stirring occasionally. Add jalapeño pepper, garlic, chili powder, cumin and salt; cook about 1 minute or until fragrant.

2. Add tomatoes, beans, water, corn and quinoa; bring to a boil. Reduce heat to low; cover and simmer 1 hour, stirring occasionally.

3. Ladle into bowls. Serve with desired toppings.

Makes 4 to 6 servings

CLASSIC LENTIL SOUP

2 tablespoons olive oil, divided

2 medium onions, chopped

1½ teaspoons salt

4 cloves garlic, minced

¼ cup tomato paste

1 teaspoon dried oregano

½ teaspoon dried basil

¼ teaspoon dried thyme

¼ teaspoon black pepper

½ cup dry sherry or white wine

8 cups vegetable broth

2 cups water

4 carrots, cut into ½-inch pieces

2 cups dried lentils, rinsed

1 cup chopped fresh parsley

1 tablespoon balsamic vinegar

1. Heat 1 tablespoon oil in large saucepan or Dutch oven over medium heat. Add onions; cook 10 minutes, stirring occasionally. Add remaining 1 tablespoon oil and salt; cook 10 minutes or until onions are golden brown, stirring frequently.

2. Add garlic; cook and stir 1 minute. Add tomato paste, oregano, basil, thyme and pepper; cook and stir 1 minute. Stir in sherry; cook 30 seconds, scraping up browned bits from bottom of saucepan.

3. Stir in broth, water, carrots and lentils; cover and bring to a boil over high heat. Reduce heat to medium-low; cook, partially covered, 30 minutes or until lentils are tender.

4. Remove from heat; stir in parsley and vinegar.

Makes 6 to 8 servings

PASTA E CECI

4 **tablespoons olive oil, divided**

1 **onion, chopped**

1 **carrot, chopped**

1 **clove garlic, minced**

1 **fresh rosemary sprig** *or* ½ **teaspoon dried rosemary**

1 **teaspoon salt**

1 **can (28 ounces) whole tomatoes, drained and crushed**

2 **cups vegetable broth or water**

1 **can (about 15 ounces) chickpeas, undrained**

⅛ **teaspoon red pepper flakes**

1 **bay leaf**

1 **cup uncooked orecchiette or medium shell pasta**

Black pepper

Chopped fresh parsley or basil (optional)

1. Heat 3 tablespoons oil in large saucepan over medium-high heat. Add onion and carrot; cook 10 minutes or until vegetables are softened, stirring occasionally.

2. Add garlic, rosemary and salt; cook and stir 1 minute. Stir in tomatoes, broth, chickpeas with liquid and red pepper flakes. Remove 1 cup mixture to food processor or blender; process until smooth. Stir back into saucepan with bay leaf; bring to a boil.

3. Stir in pasta. Reduce heat to medium; cook 12 to 15 minutes or until pasta is tender and mixture is creamy. Remove and discard bay leaf and rosemary sprig. Taste and season with additional salt and black pepper, if desired. Divide among bowls; garnish with parsley and drizzle with remaining 1 tablespoon oil.

Makes 4 servings

TIP

To easily crush the tomatoes, squeeze them one at a time between your fingers over the pot. Or coarsely chop them with a knife.

SWEET POTATO AND BLACK BEAN CHIPOTLE CHILI

1 tablespoon vegetable oil

1 large onion, chopped

2 cloves garlic, minced

2 tablespoons tomato paste

2 tablespoons chili powder

1 teaspoon ground chipotle pepper

1 teaspoon ground cumin

1 teaspoon salt

½ cup water

1 large sweet potato, peeled and cut into ½-inch pieces

1 can (28 ounces) black beans, rinsed and drained

1 can (28 ounces) crushed tomatoes

Optional toppings: sour cream, sliced green onions, shredded Cheddar cheese and tortilla strips

1. Heat oil in large saucepan over medium-high heat. Add onion; cook and stir 8 minutes or until softened and lightly browned. Add garlic, tomato paste, chili powder, chipotle pepper, cumin and salt; cook and stir 1 minute. Add water, stirring to scrape up browned bits from bottom of saucepan.

2. Add sweet potato, beans and tomatoes; bring to a boil. Reduce heat to low; simmer 30 to 40 minutes or until sweet potato is tender.

3. Ladle into bowls. Serve with desired toppings.

Makes 4 to 6 servings

Snacks

EXOTIC VEGGIE CHIPS

3 **tropical tubers (malanga, yautia, lila and/or taro roots)***

1 to 2 **green (unripe) plantains**

2 **parsnips, peeled**

1 **medium sweet potato, peeled**

1 **lotus root****

Vegetable oil, for deep frying

Salt

*These tropical tubers are all similar and their labels are frequently interchangeable or overlapping. They are available in the produce section of Latin markets. Choose whichever tubers are available and fresh. Look for firm roots without signs of mildew or soft spots.

**Lotus root is available in the produce section of Asian markets. The outside looks like a fat beige link sausage, but when sliced, the lacy, snowflake-like pattern inside is revealed.

1. Line baking sheets with paper towels.

2. Peel thick shaggy skin from tubers, rinse and dry. Thinly slice tubers and place in single layer on prepared baking sheets to absorb excess moisture. (Stack in multiple layers with paper towels between layers.) Peel thick skin from plantain. Slice and place on paper towels. Slice parsnips and sweet potato and place on paper towels. Trim lotus root and remove tough skin with paring knife. Slice and place on paper towels.

3. Fill deep fryer or large heavy skillet with 3 inches of oil; heat to 350°F on deep-fry thermometer. Working in batches, fry each vegetable until crisp and slightly curled, stirring occasionally. (Frying time will vary from 2 to 6 minutes depending on the vegetable.)

4. Remove vegetables with slotted spoon and drain on paper towels; immediately sprinkle with salt. Cool completely. Store in airtight containers at room temperature.

Makes about 6 servings

TIP

To recrisp chips, bake in preheated 350°F oven 5 minutes.

PARMESAN PICKLE CHIPS

4 large whole dill pickles (about 5 inches)

½ cup all-purpose flour

½ teaspoon salt

2 eggs

1 cup panko bread crumbs

¼ cup grated Parmesan cheese

Garlic aioli, mayonnaise or ranch dressing for dipping

1. Preheat oven to 350°F. Line baking sheet with parchment paper. Line cutting board with paper towels. Slice pickles diagonally into ¼-inch slices, place on paper towels on cutting board. Pat dry with additional paper towels to remove excess moisture.

2. Combine flour and salt in shallow bowl. Beat eggs in another shallow bowl. Combine panko and cheese in third shallow bowl.

3. Coat pickles in flour. Dip in eggs, letting excess drip back into bowl, then coat in panko. Place on prepared baking sheet.

4. Bake 15 to 20 minutes or until golden brown. Serve with desired dipping sauce.

Makes 4 servings

FRIED CAULIFLOWER WITH GARLIC TAHINI SAUCE

SAUCE

½ **cup tahini**

¼ **cup plain Greek yogurt**

2 **tablespoons lemon juice**

2 **cloves garlic, minced**

¼ **teaspoon salt**

6 **tablespoons water**

1 **tablespoon minced fresh parsley**

CAULIFLOWER

1 **cup all-purpose flour**

1½ **teaspoons salt, divided**

Pinch black pepper

4 **eggs**

¼ **cup water**

2 **cups panko bread crumbs**

1 **teaspoon ground cumin**

1 **teaspoon garlic powder**

¼ **teaspoon ground nutmeg**

1 **large head cauliflower (2½ pounds), cut into 1-inch florets**

1 **quart vegetable oil**

1. For sauce, whisk tahini, yogurt, lemon juice, garlic and ¼ teaspoon salt in medium bowl. Whisk in enough water in thin steady stream until sauce is thinned to desired consistency. Stir in parsley.

2. For cauliflower, whisk flour, ½ teaspoon salt and pepper in large bowl. Whisk eggs and ¼ cup water in medium bowl. Combine panko, remaining 1 teaspoon salt, cumin, garlic powder and nutmeg in large bowl. Toss cauliflower florets in flour mixture to coat; tap off excess. Dip in egg mixture, letting excess drain back into bowl. Place in panko mixture; toss until coated. Place breaded cauliflower on large baking sheet.

3. Line another large baking sheet with three layers of paper towels. Fill large deep saucepan with 3 inches of oil. Clip deep-fry or candy thermometer to side of pan. Heat over medium-high heat to 350°F; adjust heat to maintain temperature during frying. Add cauliflower in batches; cook 4 minutes, stirring once or twice. Remove with tongs or large slotted spoon; drain on paper towels on prepared sheet pan. Serve warm with sauce.

Makes 8 servings

TEXAS CAVIAR

1 tablespoon vegetable oil

1 cup fresh corn (from 2 to 3 ears)

2 cans (about 15 ounces each) black-eyed peas, rinsed and drained

1 can (about 15 ounces) black beans, rinsed and drained

1 cup halved grape tomatoes

1 bell pepper (any color), finely chopped

½ cup finely chopped red onion

1 jalapeño pepper, seeded and minced

2 green onions, minced

¼ cup chopped fresh cilantro

2 tablespoons red wine vinegar

1 tablespoon plus 1 teaspoon lime juice, divided

1 teaspoon salt

1 teaspoon sugar

½ teaspoon ground cumin

½ teaspoon dried oregano

2 cloves garlic, minced

¼ cup olive oil

1. Heat vegetable oil in large skillet over high heat. Add corn; cook and stir about 3 minutes or until corn is beginning to brown in spots. Place in large bowl. Add beans, tomatoes, bell pepper, red onion, jalapeño pepper, green onions and cilantro.

2. Combine vinegar, 1 tablespoon lime juice, 1 teaspoon salt, sugar, cumin, oregano and garlic in small bowl. Whisk in olive oil in thin steady stream until well blended. Pour over vegetables; stir to coat.

3. Refrigerate at least 2 hours or overnight. Just before serving, stir in remaining 1 teaspoon lime juice. Taste and season with additional salt, if desired.

Makes about 9 cups

BUFFALO CAULIFLOWER BITES

¾ cup all-purpose flour

¼ cup cornstarch

1 teaspoon salt

½ teaspoon garlic powder

¼ teaspoon black pepper

1 cup water

1 large head cauliflower (2½ pounds), cut into 1-inch florets

½ cup hot pepper sauce

¼ cup (½ stick) butter, melted

Blue cheese or ranch dressing and celery sticks for serving

1. Preheat oven to 450°F. Line large baking sheet with foil; spray with nonstick cooking spray.

2. Whisk flour, cornstarch, salt, garlic powder and black pepper in large bowl. Whisk in water until smooth and well blended. Add cauliflower to batter in batches; stir to coat. Arrange on prepared baking sheet.

3. Bake 20 minutes or until lightly browned. Combine hot pepper sauce and butter in small bowl. Pour over cauliflower; toss until well blended. Bake 5 minutes; stir. Bake 5 minutes more or until cauliflower is glazed and crisp. Serve with blue cheese dressing and celery sticks.

Makes 8 servings

ARTICHOKE PESTO DIP

1 can (14 ounces) artichoke hearts, rinsed and drained

½ cup chopped walnuts, toasted*

¼ cup packed fresh basil leaves

1 clove garlic, minced

2 tablespoons lemon juice

½ teaspoon salt

¼ cup olive oil

¼ cup grated Parmesan cheese

Pita chips

To toast walnuts, cook in medium skillet over medium heat 3 to 4 minutes or until lightly browned and fragrant, stirring frequently.

1. Place artichokes, walnuts, basil, garlic, lemon juice and salt in food processor; pulse about 12 times until coarsely chopped. With motor running, add oil in thin steady stream until smooth. Add cheese; pulse until blended.

2. Serve pesto with pita chips.

Makes 6 servings (about 1½ cups pesto)

TEX-MEX NACHOS

1 tablespoon vegetable oil

8 ounces refrigerated plant-based ground meatless product *or* 1 package (10 ounces) frozen meatless crumbles

½ cup chopped onion

2 cloves garlic, minced

2 teaspoons chili powder

1 teaspoon ground cumin

½ teaspoon salt

½ teaspoon dried oregano

1 can (about 15 ounces) kidney beans, rinsed and drained

½ cup corn

½ cup sour cream, divided

2 tablespoons mayonnaise

1 tablespoon lime juice

¼ to ½ teaspoon ground chipotle pepper

½ bag tortilla chips

½ (15-ounce) jar Cheddar cheese dip, warmed

½ cup pico de gallo

¼ cup guacamole

1 cup shredded iceberg lettuce

2 jalapeño peppers, thinly sliced into rings

1. Heat oil in large skillet over medium-high heat. Add meatless product, onion and garlic; cook and stir 6 minutes or until onion is tender, breaking up meatless product into crumbles. Add chili powder, cumin, salt and oregano; cook and stir 1 minute. Add beans and corn; reduce heat to medium-low and cook 3 minutes or until heated through.

2. For chipotle sauce, combine ¼ cup sour cream, mayonnaise, lime juice and chipotle pepper in small bowl; mix well. Place in small plastic squeeze bottle, if desired.

3. Spread tortilla chips on platter or large plate. Top with meatless mixture; drizzle with cheese dip. Top with pico de gallo, guacamole, remaining ¼ cup sour cream, lettuce and jalapeños. Squeeze or dollop chipotle sauce over nachos. Serve immediately.

Makes 4 to 6 servings

AVOCADO EGG ROLLS

DIPPING SAUCE

- ½ **cup cashew pieces**
- ½ **cup packed fresh cilantro**
- ¼ **cup honey**
- 2 **green onions, chopped**
- 2 **cloves garlic**
- 1 **tablespoon white vinegar**
- 1 **teaspoon balsamic vinegar**
- 1 **teaspoon ground cumin**
- ¼ **cup olive oil**

EGG ROLLS

- 2 **avocados, halved**
- ¼ **cup chopped drained oil-packed sun-dried tomatoes**
- 2 **tablespoons diced red onion**
- 2 **tablespoons chopped fresh cilantro**
- 1 **tablespoon lime juice**
- ¼ **teaspoon salt**
- 10 **egg roll wrappers**
  Vegetable oil for frying

1. For sauce, combine cashews, cilantro, honey, green onions, garlic, white vinegar, balsamic vinegar and cumin in food processor; process until coarsely chopped. With motor running, drizzle in olive oil in thin steady stream; process until finely chopped and well blended. Refrigerate until ready to use.

2. For egg rolls, scoop avocados into medium bowl; coarsely mash with potato masher. Stir in sun-dried tomatoes, red onion, chopped cilantro, lime juice and salt until well blended.

3. Working with one at a time, place egg roll wrapper on work surface with one corner facing you. Spread 2 tablespoons filling horizontally across wrapper. Fold short sides over filling and fold up bottom corner over filling. Moisten top edges with water; roll up egg roll, pressing to seal. Refrigerate until ready to cook.

4. Fill large deep saucepan with 2 inches of oil. Clip deep-fry or candy thermometer to side of pan. Heat over medium-high heat to 350°F; adjust heat to maintain temperature during frying. Cook egg rolls in batches about 3 minutes or until golden brown, turning once. Drain on paper towel-lined plate. Cut egg rolls in half diagonally; serve with sauce.

Makes 10 egg rolls and 1 cup sauce

CAULIFLOWER SOCCA

2 cups chickpea flour (besan)

1¾ teaspoons salt

¼ teaspoon black pepper

2 cups water

½ cup olive oil, divided

1½ cups finely chopped cauliflower

1 can (about 15 ounces) chickpeas, rinsed and drained

2 tablespoons chopped fresh cilantro or parsley

1. Whisk chickpea flour, salt and pepper in large bowl to remove any lumps. Whisk in water and ¼ cup oil. Let stand at room temperature at least 30 minutes.

2. Meanwhile, preheat oven to 450°F. Place large (12-inch) cast iron skillet in oven to preheat at least 10 minutes. Pour remaining ¼ cup oil into hot skillet. Add cauliflower and chickpeas. Bake 10 minutes.

3. Whisk cilantro into batter; pour batter over cauliflower and chickpeas in skillet. Bake 15 minutes or until edge is lightly browned, top is firm and toothpick inserted into center comes out with moist crumbs. Cut into wedges; serve warm or at room temperature.

Makes 8 servings

Index

Index

METRIC CONVERSION CHART

VOLUME MEASUREMENTS (dry)

1/8 teaspoon = 0.5 mL
1/4 teaspoon = 1 mL
1/2 teaspoon = 2 mL
3/4 teaspoon = 4 mL
1 teaspoon = 5 mL
1 tablespoon = 15 mL
2 tablespoons = 30 mL
1/4 cup = 60 mL
1/3 cup = 75 mL
1/2 cup = 125 mL
2/3 cup = 150 mL
3/4 cup = 175 mL
1 cup = 250 mL
2 cups = 1 pint = 500 mL
3 cups = 750 mL
4 cups = 1 quart = 1 L

VOLUME MEASUREMENTS (fluid)

1 fluid ounce (2 tablespoons) = 30 mL
4 fluid ounces (1/2 cup) = 125 mL
8 fluid ounces (1 cup) = 250 mL
12 fluid ounces (1 1/2 cups) = 375 mL
16 fluid ounces (2 cups) = 500 mL

WEIGHTS (mass)

1/2 ounce = 15 g
1 ounce = 30 g
3 ounces = 90 g
4 ounces = 120 g
8 ounces = 225 g
10 ounces = 285 g
12 ounces = 360 g
16 ounces = 1 pound = 450 g

DIMENSIONS

1/16 inch = 2 mm
1/8 inch = 3 mm
1/4 inch = 6 mm
1/2 inch = 1.5 cm
3/4 inch = 2 cm
1 inch = 2.5 cm

OVEN TEMPERATURES

250°F = 120°C
275°F = 140°C
300°F = 150°C
325°F = 160°C
350°F = 180°C
375°F = 190°C
400°F = 200°C
425°F = 220°C
450°F = 230°C

BAKING PAN SIZES

Utensil	Size in Inches/Quarts	Metric Volume	Size in Centimeters
Baking or Cake Pan (square or rectangular)	8×8×2	2 L	20×20×5
	9×9×2	2.5 L	23×23×5
	12×8×2	3 L	30×20×5
	13×9×2	3.5 L	33×23×5
Loaf Pan	8×4×3	1.5 L	20×10×7
	9×5×3	2 L	23×13×7
Round Layer Cake Pan	8×1½	1.2 L	20×4
	9×1½	1.5 L	23×4
Pie Plate	8×1¼	750 mL	20×3
	9×1¼	1 L	23×3
Baking Dish or Casserole	1 quart	1 L	—
	1½ quart	1.5 L	—
	2 quart	2 L	—